Scamper On

Games for Imagination Development

D1379567

By Bob Eberle

PRUFROCK PRESS INC.

Because of the tremendous popularity of *Scamper*, Bob Eberle, the author, was urged by teachers, students, and imaginative adults to create another book of games to encourage the creative-imaginative expression of children. *Scamper On* was the result. In *Scamper On* the focus of the games moves upward from the primary games to serve a general audience.

There is a smooth and logical flow of activities from the first book to the second book. Almost without exception, those who have used one book, want the other.

Table of Contents

"The best thinking seems to integrate the two ways of knowing. By providing fantasies and our usual verbal information, we give students experience in combining these two modes of thinking and knowing."

—The Second Centering Book

Acknowledgements

With sincere appreciation, acknowledgement is made to those individuals who made recommendations, critiqued the manuscript, and otherwise made helpful suggestions. Their suggestions and recommendations were graciously received, and freely used in preparing the format and content of this work.

Karen Agne	Berenice Bleedorn
Jeanne Brunworth	Starr Cline
Jo Doersam	Carol Downing
Pat Doyle	Gretchen Duling
Kathy Gerber	Jodie Grinter
Jean Helm	Jennine Jackson
Bobbie Kraver	Phyllis McDonald
DeAnne McConnel	Helen C. Mitchell
Ruth B. Noller	Sidney J. Parnes
Bev Schaake	Doris J. Shallcross
Bob Stanish	Nancy J. Smith
Nancy Suhre	Pansy Torrance
Shirley Ward	Carol Wittig

Why *Scamper On?*

To be honest, it had not been my intention to write a follow-up to the *Scamper* book. You may ask, "If it was not your intention, why did you do it?" There are reasons, and I will share them with you.

In recent years, new and exciting information concerning the functioning of the mind has been made available. Fundamentally, each of us has two minds which are referred to as brain hemispheres. We have learned that each hemisphere of the brain has its own unique functions. Learning how to orchestrate the activities of both hemispheres, and knowing how to play inter-active, harmonious, intellectual tunes, is of primary importance in the development of total human potential. This, then, becomes an objective of *Scamper On.*

Teacher friends, particularly those in the Williamsville, NY, area, have convinced me of the need to write a follow-up. Their comment has been, "Bob, our cardboard boxes have worn out. Won't you give us something more to *Scamper* with?" In meeting the requests of teachers and adult trainers, the focus of the games has moved upward from the primary games to serve a general audience.

Being known as Mr. Scamper to school children is a source of satisfaction. The letters and comments received from children are both rewarding and motivating. There is the typed note from Matt over in Indiana. He suggests that a game be written about robots. It is for Matt, his friends, his teachers, and for imaginative adults, that I extend the invitation to *Scamper On.*

—Bob Eberle
Edwardsville, IL

What's in the Word *Scamper?*

Literally, the word scamper means "to run playfully about, as a child." Scamper is a descriptive word, it pictures the playful search for ideas and images that the games are designed to bring about. It is also an acronym. Each of the seven letters of the word SCAMPER serves as the initial letter of word phrases that form an idea-spurring checklist. This checklist is the foundation of both *Scamper* and *Scamper On*.

Serving as a point of reference, a checklist provokes the mind and spurs the production of ideas. Open-ended in nature, checklisting questions ask "What if?" and "How about?" The intention is to run the scale of possibilities in search of creative ideas that may lead to the solution of problems. The more ideas, the better. According to J. P. Guilford, "The person who is capable of producing a large number of ideas per unit, has a greater chance of having significant ideas."

There are two aspects of the *Scamper Checklist* that are worthy of mention. First, it has general application. It may be used in planning a dinner party, organizing a vacation, disciplining children, or meeting a challenge on the job. When problems and challenges arise, *Scamper* with them. Secondly, the checklist prompts a large variety of mental manipulations associated with creative thinking. In the minds of inventors, composers, designers, and artists, the manipulative techniques lead to novel, original, and useful products and ideas. All of these techniques are woven into the *Scamper* and *Scamper On* games.

Scamper Checklist

S	**Substitute**	To have a person or thing act or serve in the place of another. Who else? What else? Other place? Time?
C	**Combine**	To bring together, to unite. Combine what? Bring whom together? Combine purposes? Ideas? Materials?
A	**Adjust**	To adjust for the purpose of suiting a condition. Reshape? Tune-up? Tone-down? Accommodate? Agree?
M	**Modify**	To alter, to change the form or quality. Other color? Sound? Motion? Form? Size? Shape? Taste? Odor?
	Magnify	To enlarge, to make greater in form or quality. Add what to make higher? Stronger? Thicker? Longer?
	Minify	To make less, to minimize. Make what smaller? Lighter? Slower? Less frequent? Shrink? Reduce?
P	**Put to Other Uses**	Use for purpose other than originally intended. New uses as is? Other places to use? Use when? How?
E	**Eliminate**	To remove, omit, or get rid of a quality. What to cut out? Remove? Simplify? Weed out?
R	**Reverse**	To place opposite or contrary. To turn what around? Upside down? Inside out? 180° flip?
	Rearrange	Change order or sequence. Other pattern? Layout? Plan? Scheme? Regroup? Redistribute?

Instructions for *Scamper On* Game Leaders

It takes two to *Scamper*, a game leader and a child of any age. (Adults have been known to *Scamper*.) The leader may serve an individual or a group numbering up to 100.

To play the games, the leader reads the script paying close attention to the required pauses indicated by the three dots (. . .). The purpose of the pause is to provide time for the players to carry out the cues and directions given by the leader.

During the pause the leader should observe the expressions, reactions, and gestures of players. *Remember, the three dots are your signal to wait and watch.*

Thinking and visualizing takes time. You will know when to continue the game when players nod, smile, or otherwise indicate their participation.

The games should be played with enthusiasm and anticipation. This places a requirement on the leader. The enthusiasm of the leader sets the pace and establishes the emotional tone of the games.

Within the structure of the games, ample opportunity is provided for the leader to express his or her own creative imagination. Leaders may modify the games to suit a particular group. *Improvisation is encouraged.*

Before Playing the *Scamper* Games

Acquaint yourself with the contents. Take time to read the *Appendix. The Scamper Model for Creative Imagination Development*, which appears on page 37, describes the rationale upon which the games have been designed.

Notice that varying styles have been used in writing the games. Levels of abstractness and divergent thinking are increased as the games progress.

Understand that the games do not have to be played from beginning to end. Break points may be established depending on the time available and the interest level of the players.

Check the *Follow-up Activities* that are found after each game. Determine which activities are appropriate for your group of players. Add some activities of your own.

After reading the *Directions for Playing*, refine the expression you will use when introducing the games to players.

Read the first two games as if you were actually playing them. Take time to pause, as indicated, and picture the images you are directing. Timing yourself during this activity may be helpful.

Directions for Playing the *Scamper On* Games (To be read aloud)

We are going to play a game called *Scamper On*. This is a pretend game. When we pretend, we use our imaginations and see pictures in our minds. Using our imagination and seeing pictures in our mind is a fun thing to do. Listen while I read the rules to you.

Rules of the Game

I will tell you about something and ask you to think about it . . . to pretend to see it in your imagination.

Sometimes, I will ask you to do something . . . You may nod your head *yes*, or shake your head *no*.

The best way to pretend is to close your eyes. Place your feet on the floor, drop your arms into your lap, then sit quietly and relaxed.

At times, I may ask you to think up some ideas. When I do, let the ideas flow into your mind and see them in your imagination.

Try hard to see mental images. The harder you try, the better pictures you will see.

(It may be necessary to review the rules before playing each game.)

Yellow Jell-O

➡ We are going to play a practice game. Are you ready? . . .
⇨ Are your eyes closed? . . .
⇨ Nod your head *yes* if you are ready and your eyes are closed . . .
⇨ Good. Pretend that a dish of yellow Jell-O is sitting on a table in front of you . . .
⇨ Do you see it? . . .
⇨ Nod your head *yes* if you see it . . .
⇨ Put a spoon on the table beside the dish of jell-o . . .
⇨ Pick up the spoon and take a bite of Jell-O . . .
⇨ Take another bite and squish it around in your mouth . . .
⇨ Do you taste the flavor? . . .
⇨ Put a big gob of whipped cream on top of the Jell-O . . .
⇨ Sprinkle some toasted coconut on the whipped cream and place a big red cherry on top of it . . .
⇨ Take a good look at your dish of Jell-O . . .
⇨ Take your spoon and have a few more bites . . .
⇨ Stop eating . . .
➡ Like magic, your dish is now empty . . .
⇨ Soon, you will have another dish of Jell-O, but it will not be yellow. What color will you make it? . . .
⇨ Make it that color . . .
⇨ Is there something you would like to put in your Jell-O? . . .
⇨ Put it in . . .
⇨ Is there something you would like to put on top of the Jell-O? . . .
⇨ Put it on . . .
⇨ Take your spoon and eat a bite of Jell-O . . .
⇨ Squish it around and taste the flavor . . .
⇨ Take one more bite and you're finished . . . (Call for a discussion.)

Eighth Day of the Week

"There are not enough days in the week!" Did you ever hear anyone say that? If so, they were saying that there is not enough time to do what they want to do or need to do. If we use our imagination, there might be a way to solve that problem. Let's pretend that there are eight days in every week. The extra day would come after Sunday and before Monday. The eighth day would have to have a name. It might work to use a name that describes the things we would do on that day. Let's try it and see what happens.

➡ Dream along and make a day that you would spend with others. In your mind, think of people who you would like to be with . . .
  ➪ Now that you have some people in mind, choose some of them to be with you on the eighth day of the week . . .
  ➪ Fine. Now that you have some people to spend time with you, you will need to think of things that all of you would like to do together. Think of those things . . .
  ➪ See yourself and your friends doing those things . . .
  ➪ We'll call it *Friends Day*.

Here's another idea. Let's say that the eighth day of the week is set aside to go to places that we want to go. That would be a great idea.

➡ Think of all the places in the world that you would like to visit, then narrow it down to one place . . .
  ➪ Do you have it? . . . Good! Now get on an airplane, settle back, and enjoy your flight. You are above the clouds flying along . . .
  ➪ Your plane is now coming in for a landing . . .
  ➪ Leave the plane, walk around, meet people, go shopping, and sightseeing . . .
  ➪ Your visit is over. Get aboard the plane and get ready to fly home. You are now flying along and heading home . . .
  ➪ It touches down . . .
  ➪ You are now back home. Today is *Fly Day*.

It has turned out to be a very warm day. You really should go outdoors and enjoy the sunshine.

➡ There are many things to do outside on a warm, sunshiny day.
  ➪ Make a list in your mind of things to do . . .

⇨ You have all day to do these things. Choose some of them, and then see yourself doing them . . .

⇨ Better take time out now for a cold drink. Pretend that you have a cool drink. Sip it slowly and enjoy it . . .

⇨ What day is it? Of course, it's *Thirst Day*.

Remember, we said that the eighth day of the week could be spent doing things that we didn't get done the first seven days. Think back.

➡ What are some things that didn't get done? . . .
   ⇨ You could do them now in your imagination. Find something to do, and do it in your imagination . . .
   ⇨ Do you feel better now that you have gotten it out of the way? You can get caught up any old *When's Day*.
➡ Today is *Two's Day*. Everything happens in two's.
   ⇨ Sit down for breakfast and eat two of everything . . .
   ⇨ Have a happy *Two's Day*.
➡ Today is your day to do nothing. Nothing, but sit in your yard dreaming and listening to the sounds around you.
   ⇨ About half asleep, you hear the birds singing . . .
   ⇨ Down the block a dog is barking . . .
   ⇨ Across town a church bell is ringing . . .
   ⇨ A kitten jumps up beside you, brushes your face, and purrs in your ear . . .
   ⇨ The sounds of nature are all around you . . .
   ⇨ Listen, do you hear that siren? . . .
   ⇨ It is coming closer . . .
   ⇨ It turns down your street . . .
   ⇨ Jump up and see what is happening . . .
   ⇨ You knew it all the time, it's *Sounds Day*.
➡ There are many things that have a pleasing aroma. To name a few you might mention perfume, bread baking in the oven, or a bouquet of flowers.
   ⇨ Think of things that have a pleasing aroma, as you place them one by one on a long table . . .
   ⇨ Think hard and place some more things on the long table . . .
   ⇨ Now you have a smellgasboard. Starting at the front of the line, take a whiff of everything as you go along the line . . .
   ⇨ What else? It's *Smells Day!*

Follow-up activities:

⇨ Call on players to invent their own "eighth day of the week" and then write a game scenario.

⇨ Selecting any one of the day titles, call on students to use it as a title for a rhyme or poem.

Scamper
calendar

IMAGINARY

Sunday	FUNDAY	Monday	Tuesday	Wednesday	Thursday	Friday	Saturday
		1	2	3	4	5	6
7	8	9	10	11	12	13	14
15	16	17	18	19	20	21	22
23	24	25	26	27	28	29	30
31	32						

Sights and Sounds, Upside Down, and All Around

It is likely that game leaders will not wish to use all of the many parts of this game in one session. It is recommended that you be selective and group the parts for two or more sessions.

When you want it to, your mind can work magic. You can direct your mind to think about something that happened years ago. If you try, you can see a picture in your mind of the things that happened. If you wish, you can direct your mind to the future. When you do, you are able to think about and see images of events that might happen five to 10 years from now. When you turn the magic on, you are also able to see and hear things that may never happen. Turn your magic on and see some things that may never happen.

⇨ Back and forth swim the fish in the sea . . .
  Watch as they decorate their Christmas tree . . .
⇨ Your breakfast food box is full of prunes . . .
  Open the flap and it plays a tune . . .
⇨ Both boys and girls have yellow curls . . .
  They shake their heads and a flag unfurls . . .
⇨ Off you go for a walk in the sky . . .
  Stop at the corner for a burger and fries . . .
⇨ Cats and rats are very fat . . .
  They are dressed in clothes and wearing hats . . .
⇨ Rivers are yellow, then green, then brown . . .
  Fill your glass with soda and drink it down . . .
⇨ The birds you see will flutter and fly . . .
  Then stop at traffic signals in the sky . . .
⇨ Turn on the TV set that is in your head . . .
  Watch your favorite program while lying in bed . . .
⇨ Take a space ship out of your pocket . . .
  Send it flying like a rocket . . .
⇨ Dogs and hogs are spinning a log . . .
  Put them on land and send them to jog . . .
⇨ What you think will turn to stone . . .
  At the end of the day a mountain has grown . . .

➦ Look around for a place to hide . . .
  No place to go, so vanish inside . . .
➦ Doughnuts are square and full of air . . .
  Two dollars a dozen at the county fair . . .
➦ You are going up-up-up, in a hot air balloon . . .
  Your pilot is a hairy baboon . . .
➦ Look in a mirror and see a frown . . .
  Notice your eyeballs are hanging down . . .
➦ The wumbas and wampas come walking by . . .
  Give them wings and teach them to fly . . .
➦ Your favorite meal is on the table . . .
  Feed it to the horse out in the stable . . .
➦ Listen close and bells will chime . . .
  Listen far and words will rhyme. . .
➦ With vision and hope for good times ahead . . .
  The sun will beam down on your pretty head . . .

Follow-up activities:

➦ Organize players in groups of two. As games are repeated, partners take turns describing aloud, and in great detail, the visions that they are experiencing. Players may be given the opportunity to call for games of their choice.
➦ Working in small groups, or in a large group, players may be asked to tell what led up to the game event. Other players may then be asked to tell what happened as a result of the event.

Brown Paper Bags

What is it that you bring home from the store, never eat, and end up throwing away? . . . The answer is brown paper grocery bags. Brown paper bags are useful, but they are dull and not very exciting. It would pep up our day if grocery bags were made in bright colors.

➡ Let's try that idea in our imagination. Pretend that a brown paper bag is sitting on the table in front of you . . .
   ⮕ Do you see it? Good. Take another look at the brown bag . . .
   ⮕ Now make your bag a friendly orange color . . .
   ⮕ Make it a cheerful green color . . .
   ⮕ Make it a peppy yellow color . . .
   ⮕ What would a friendly, cheerful, peppy bag look like? Make your bag look just like that . . .
➡ Using our imagination we can pretend and do many wonderful things with a paper bag. First, let's make some improvements . . .
   ⮕ To start, put a handle on it . . .
   ⮕ Give it a lid or a cover . . .
   ⮕ Put a flap pocket on the side . . .
   ⮕ Put your name on it in big black letters . . .
   ⮕ Make a place for a radio in the handle . . .
   ⮕ Give it three bright colors, then stand back and look at it. . .
   ⮕ Are there any improvements you would like to make on your bag? If so, go ahead and make them . . .
   ⮕ Now, how do you like your bag? . . .
➡ Take another brown bag. On the side of it write *Bother's Bag*. You will use the *Bother's Bag* to collect things that give you trouble. You might also wish to collect things that are worn out, broken, too small, or anything you wish to get rid of.
   ⮕ Now one by one, see the things you want to put in the bag, then put them in . . .
   ⮕ Keep putting things that bother you into the bag . . .
   ⮕ Now pick up the *Bother's Bag* and shake it . . .
   ⮕ The bag is empty. The things that bothered you and gave you trouble have disappeared . . .
   ⮕ Make a place for a radio in the handle . . .
   ⮕ Give it three bright colors, then stand back and look at it. . .

- ➪ Are there any improvements you would like to make on your bag? If so, go ahead and make them . . .
- ➪ Now, how do you like your bag? . . .
➡ Take another brown bag and write on it *Boodle Bag*. In the bag you will collect a Boodle of things that you wish for. One by one make a wish for something. Then, reach in the Boodle Bag and pull it out.
- ➪ Start wishing . . .
- ➪ The bag is not empty, keep on wishing and pulling things out of the bag . . .
- ➪ Isn't it wonderful, the things you can do with your imagination? . . .
➡ Going on, there are some improvements we can make on the Brown Paper Bag. First, make it a heavy-duty, strong, white plastic bag . . .
- ➪ Look at the bag now . . .
- ➪ Make it air tight and water tight . . .
- ➪ Make it much larger . . .
- ➪ Make it much smaller . . .
- ➪ Turn it inside out, Use scissors to cut around the open end to make a fringe . . .
- ➪ Pretend you have made the bag into a white-fringed rain hat . . . and see how it looks . . .
➡ Using your imagination, you can create all kinds of things out of a white plastic bag. I will name some things. Your task will be to make them out of a plastic bag and see them in your imagination. Ready? . . .
- ➪ Make a rain coat for a dog . . .
- ➪ Make a trampoline and bounce on it . . .
- ➪ Make a kite and fly it . . .
- ➪ Put a handle on it and make a fly swatter . . .
- ➪ Make a shade and put it on a lamp . . .
- ➪ Make a parachute and float down to earth . . .
- ➪ Make a poster and hang it on he wall . . .
- ➪ Buy some goldfish and carry them home in your bag . . .
A white plastic bag is a neat thing to have. You can make many kinds of things out of a white plastic bag.
➡ Now it is your turn to think of some things to make out of the bag, and to find some new ways of using it. In what ways might you use the bag if you were going for a hike in the woods? Think of some ways and see them in your imagination . . .
- ➪ Do it now . . .
- ➪ Ways to use it in the kitchen? . . .

➪ Ways to use it with pets? . . .
➪ Ways to use it with sports? . . .
➪ Ways to use it on a picnic? . . .
➪ If you think of other ways to use the bag, write them down so you don't forget them. You may have a valuable idea.

Follow-up activities:
➪ Conduct a discussion in which players tell the uses they made of the plastic bag.
➪ Using a bag, brick, tin can, or coat hanger, apply each step of the *Scamper* technique in a brainstorm for other uses.

Dogs and Cats and Hogs and Bats

In this game, you will use your magic mind viewer. When you look into your viewer, like magic you will see a picture of those things that you bring into your mind. The pictures you see will be in color and very clear. The harder you try to see the colored picture, the clearer it will be. Are you ready to try out your magic mind viewer? Fine, Let's get started.

➡ Looking into your viewer you will see a picture of a dog. It can be any kind of dog that you want to make it . . .
　➪ Look now and see a dog . . .
　➪ Now that you have a picture of a dog, look to see what it is that makes this animal different from other animals . . .
　➪ Do you have it? . . .
　➪ Remember it . . .
➡ Next, look into your viewer and see a cat. Make it any kind of cat that you wish to make it . . .
　➪ Look now and see the cat . . .
　➪ Now, we wish to see what it is that makes this animal different from all other kinds of animals . . .
　➪ Look now to see the ways in which it is different . . .
　➪ Remember what it is that makes the cat different . . .
➡ If you were to visit a farm, you might see a hog. If you look now, you will see a hog in your viewer . . .
　➪ Look at the hog . . .
　➪ Look again and see what it is that makes this animal different from all others . . .
　➪ Remember the things that make the hog different . . .
➡ Have you ever seen a bat flying around in early evening? Bats are very unusual . . .
　➪ Make a bat stop flying and see it in your viewer . . .
　➪ Look to see how this creature is different from all others . . .
　➪ Do you have it? . . .
　➪ Remember it . . .
➡ Now it is time to turn the magic on. When you turn on the magic, your viewer can show you a picture of things that do not exist . . .
　➪ Let's try it by starting with a dog and a cat . . .
　➪ Remember the things that made these animals different from all others? . . .
　➪ Taking these things, you are going to put them on one animal . . .

⇨ Look now, and see a Dogcat . . .

⇨ In one picture you see an animal that looks like a dog and a cat . . .

⇨ Try to remember what it looks like . . .

➡ Going on, we'll see what other kinds of magic we might work . . .

⇨ Remember the things that made a hog and a bat different? . . .

⇨ You are going to use those things now . . .

⇨ Turn on your viewer and see a Hogbat . . .

⇨ Remember the picture of your Hogbat . . .

➡ You have a picture of both a Dogcat and a Hogbat . . .

⇨ Taking both of your pictures, combine them to make one picture . . .

⇨ Look into your viewer and see a Hogdog Catbat . . .

⇨ Keep looking . . .

⇨ Try to see a part of each of the four animals . . .

➡ Now, I am going to give you some things about other animals that make them different from all others. Your task will be to take what I give you and try it on some other animals . . .

⇨ Take the stripes of a zebra and put them on another animal . . .

⇨ You should be seeing an animal with zebra stripes . . .

⇨ Take the tusks of an elephant and give them to another animal . . .

⇨ Take a monkey's tail and give it to another animal . . .

⇨ Take the horns of a Texas steer and give them to another animal . . .

⇨ When you use your imagination and your mind viewer, you can make things happen like magic.

Follow-up activities:

⇨ Call on players to draw pictures of any of the animals they created.

⇨ Have four players make a team drawing. Each will use one of the animals in the title.

⇨ In each of the above activities, have the players give a new and original name to the animal that they created.

⇨ In each of the first two activities, have the players compose a story telling why this animal didn't make it to Noah's Ark.

⇨ Have one player describe an animal while the second draws it.

⇨ Any of the animals created may be the focus of a jingle, rhyme, or poem.

⇨ Using the *combination technique*, have players apply it to fruit, games, automobiles, colors, and sounds.

⇨ Encourage players to give elaborate descriptions and make elaborate drawings. Have them tell a complete and detailed story.

Mindshower

A *mindshower* is not quite the same as a brainstorm. When a group of people produce a large number of ideas for solving a problem, they are brainstorming. When one or more people capture ideas in their mind and show them as images, it is called a *mindshower*. So you might say that a *mindshower* pours ideas, and then shows them to you. Inventors, composers, and artists often use *mindshowers* to create new, useful, and imaginative products.

➡ Checklisting is one of the ways you can start a *mindshower.* Starting with the first letter of the alphabet, I will name some things that start with the letter **A**. Shower pictures in your mind as I call them out . . .
  ➪ Apple . . .
  ➪ Ape . . .
  ➪ Angel . . .
  ➪ Airplane . . .
  ➪ Asteroid . . .
  ➪ Antlers . . .
  ➪ Armadillo . . .
  ➪ Automobile . . .
  ➪ Art . . .

➡ Now that you have showered pictures of things starting with **A**, we'll go on to invent some things that you have never seen or thought of before. They will be different. Do your best to picture them in your mind. Are you ready? . . .
  ➪ See an antlers angel . . .
  ➪ See an apple asteroid . . .
  ➪ See an airplane arm . . .
  ➪ See an ape automobile . . .
  ➪ See an angel apple . . .
  ➪ See an armadillo automobile . . .
  ➪ See an asteroid ant . . .
  ➪ See an airplane automobile . . .

➡ Now we will go to the letter **B** and use it to shower some things that are good to eat, see, taste, and smell. See the **B** things as I give them to you . . .
  ➪ Baked beans . . .
  ➪ Brown bread . . .
  ➪ Burgers . . .
  ➪ Buttered beets . . .

⇨ Bacon . . .

⇨ Broccoli . . .

⇨ Bologna . . .

⇨ Biscuits . . .

⇨ Beefsteak . . .

⇨ Blueberries . . .

⇨ Boiled bullfrogs . . .

⇨ Bubbly beverages . . .

⇨ Brazed bison . . .

⇨ Butterscotch bagels . . .

⇨ Big bananas . . .

➡ There are many good things to eat that begin with the letter **B**. See, touch, smell, and taste these combinations as I give them to you . . .

⇨ Butterscotch banana brown bread . . .

⇨ Brazed bullfrog burgers . . .

⇨ Bubbly blueberry beverage . . .

⇨ Bacon bits buttered broccoli . . .

⇨ Boiled bologna bagels . . .

⇨ Bacon baked beans on big buns . . .

⇨ Did you find a combination that you really liked? . . . Remember it and be ready to tell about it.

➡ Go on to the letter **C**. We'll try another kind of *mindshower*. I will give you the name of a business. You will see the uniform that the people in this business wear. On the front of the uniform is an emblem, patch, or design. The design will let everyone know what kind of business the person is in. Are there any questions? . . . As I give you the kinds of businesses, see the uniform, and see the emblem . . .

⇨ Car rental company . . .

⇨ Carry-out food store . . .

⇨ Clock shop . . .

⇨ Computer store . . .

⇨ Cat hospital . . .

⇨ Cheese shop . . .

⇨ Cold storage locker plant . . .

⇨ Carpet cleaners . . .

⇨ Clothing store . . .

With all of these designs in mind, you should be ready to create some unusual emblems. If you have a favorite, keep it in mind . . .

➡ In playing the **D** game, we'll try yet another kind of *mindshower*. When I name something that begins with the letter **D**, you will try to see a picture in your mind in three dimensions. You will not only see the height and width of something, you will also see the depth. Your mind picture will be better than a colored photograph. Here we go on the 3-D photographs . . .

⇨ A black and white spotted dalmatian dog . . .

⇨ A deep sea diver . . .

⇨ A detective wearing a disguise . . .

⇨ A deserted desert . . .

⇨ A down-hearted donkey . . .

That will be all for the **D's**. Remember which photograph you liked best.

Follow-up activities: (**Note:** when using the follow-up activities, each letter game may make up a session.)

⇨ Ask, "Did anything unusual happen when you were playing the *Mindshower Game*?" Allow players to share their experiences.

⇨ Following any of the given formats, call on players to write their own games using other letters of the alphabet.

⇨ With reference to the **C** Game, have players draw any kind of emblem they wish. Other players are then given the opportunity to guess the kind of business or work represented.

⇨ With any of the games, form pairs and have each person describe an image in detail leaving nothing to the imagination of the listener.

Leap Before You Look

Looking before leaping is usually a good thing to do. By taking a look first, you are able to avoid problems that could turn out to be serious. When you pretend, and use your imagination, you don't have to worry about getting your bones broken, or your head split open. It is safe to take a risk and *Leap Before You Look*. In playing this make-believe game, you will take giant leaps in your imagination and land in many strange and wonderful places.

I will give you the command to leap. When I say *Leap*, blast-off like a silver rocket streaking orange fire and billowing steamy white clouds. As you zoom through space, I will tell you where you are about to land. After a soft landing, you will have time to visit and see the sights. When it is time to end your visit, I will give you the command *Return to Home Base*. Are there any questions? . . . Now, please listen to the instructions as you prepare to take a giant leap into space.

➡ Ready? . . . Leave the earth behind you and leap high into space . . .
  ⇨ Notice that your body feels lighter as you go higher and higher . . .
  ⇨ The earth becomes smaller as you float upward . . .
  ⇨ Now you are approaching Galactic I, the first city in space . . .
  ⇨ The gate opens, and you walk into the sparkling clean city . . .
  ⇨ The people you meet are friendly and anxious to talk to you . . .
  ⇨ Ask them why everyone is wearing a brightly colored uniform . . .
  ⇨ Take a last look around as you prepare to *Return to Home Base* . . .
  ⇨ Say bye to your new friends, then float back to Earth . . .
  ⇨ Touch down at home base . . .
➡ Get ready to take another leap . . .
  ⇨ Are you ready? . . .
  ⇨ Leap high into the air . . .
  ⇨ Now, slowly tumble back to earth . . .
  ⇨ You have landed on a raft and are floating down a river . . .
  ⇨ Get comfortable, then view all there is to view as you float along . . .
  ⇨ From downstream a boat moves closer to you . . .
  ⇨ Wave back to the people who are waving to you . . .
  ⇨ Over to your right you can see a town in the distance . . .
  ⇨ As you get closer, the buildings get larger . . .
  ⇨ You decide to stop at the town and look for a place to land . . .
  ⇨ Stretch, look around, and get ready to *Return to Home Base* . . .
  ⇨ Touch down at home base . . .

19

➡ Get ready to leap . . .
  ⇨ Leap . . .
  ⇨ You are landing in a country far, far away . . .
  ⇨ You are in a strange city, and strange people are all around you . . .
  ⇨ Walk down the street and look into the store windows . . .
  ⇨ Stop at a restaurant and order your lunch . . .
  ⇨ Thank your waitress and taste your lunch . . .
  ⇨ Do you like it? . . .
  ⇨ If you do, finish your lunch and pay for it . . .
  ⇨ Walk out of the restaurant and *Return to Home Base* . . .
  ⇨ Touch down . . .

➡ It is leap time again. Get ready to leap. . . .
  ⇨ Leap . . .
  ⇨ You come down through billowy dark clouds and the day is wet and windy . . .
  ⇨ You find yourself alone in a dimly lit hallway of a deserted castle . . .
  ⇨ Mist is rolling down the hallway toward you . . .
  ⇨ As you look and listen, you hear strange sounds . . .
  ⇨ As the mist comes closer . . .
  ⇨ You see a ghost in front of you . . .
  ⇨ Talk to the ghost, try to find out something about it . . .
  ⇨ Now a dazzling bright light appears down the hallway . . .
  ⇨ It gets brighter and brighter . . .
  ⇨ It is time to leave the castle and *Return to Home Base* . . .
  ⇨ Touch down at home base . . .

Follow-up activities:

⇨ Call on players to share the senses experienced in each of the games: Sound—Taste—Touch—Sight—Odors.
⇨ Call on players to picture a life-like experience in any of the games and describe it in detail.
⇨ Call on players to make a drawing of the most vivid vision that they experienced in any of the games.
⇨ Two or more players may be used to write a scenario, and then act it out.
⇨ The leader may take players on a blind leap without a designated place to land. Players are then free to land any place they wish. The experiences of the blind leap may be used to write a short story.

Oops!

The word *Oops* is used to express surprise. When things take a turn away from the expected, we may respond by saying *Oops!* In the game that you are about to play, *Oops* will be used as a watchword that tells you to complete a rhyme on your own. You will picture the rhyme in your imagination and then go on to invent an unexpected ending. There will be no wrong answers. See an ending that will be unusual, clever, and one of a kind. Close your eyes and be ready to see the rhyme and give it an ending.

Note: Each rhyme may be played as a single game. Determine the number of games you wish to play per session. Provide extra time for thinking and seeing.

All of the *Scamper* techniques may be applied when playing this game. When introducing this game, you may wish to review the techniques represented by the letters of the acronym.

⇨ Little Polly Flanders . . .
Sat among the cinders . . .
Oops! . . .

⇨ Dickory, dickory dare . . .
The pig flew up in the air . . .
Oops! . . .

⇨ Jack and Jill went up the hill . . .
To fetch a pail of water . . .
Jack fell down . . .
Oops! . . .

⇨ Old Mother Twitchett had but one eye . . .
And a long tail which she let fly . . .
And every time she went through a gap . . .
Oops! . . .

⇨ Wee Willie Winkie runs through the town . . .
Upstairs and downstairs in his nightgown . . .
Oops! . . .

⇨ There was a man in our town, . . .
And he was wondrous wise . . .
He jumped into a bramble bush . . .
Oops! . . .

⇨ Little Miss Muffet . . .
  Sat on a Tuffet . . .
  Eating her curds and whey . . .
  There came a big spider . . .
  and *Oops!* . . .
⇨ Humpty Dumpty sat on a wall . . .
  Humpty Dumpty had a great fall . . .
  Oops! . . .
⇨ Old Mother Hubbard . . .
  Went to the cupboard . . .
  To get her poor dog a bone . . .
  But when she got there . . .
  Oops! . . .
⇨ There were once two cats of Kilkenny . . .
  Each thought there was one cat too many . . .
  Oops! . . .
⇨ Hey diddle, diddle! . . .
  The cat and the fiddle . . .
  The cow jumped over the moon . . .
  Oops! . . .
⇨ I saw a ship a-sailing . . .
  A-sailing on the sea . . .
  And, Oh! It was all laden . . .
  With pretty things for thee . . .
  Oops! . . .
⇨ There was a fat man of Bombay . . .
  Smoking his pipe one sunshiny day . . .
  When a bird called a snipe. . .
  Oops! . . .

Follow-up activity:

⇨ Taking the rhymes one at a time, call on players to write their own original endings. Players may also be called on to compose their own
  rhymes making provision for an *Oops!* ending.

23

Room for the Future

Using your imagination, you are able to make plans and see things ahead of time. When you direct your mind to think and create images, you are able to design the future just the way you want it to be. In the game we are about to play, you will be using your mind to plan, see, and design the future. You will plan your own room, then you will picture it in your mind.

To do this, you will design parts of the room one at a time. Then, you will take the parts and join them together as you plan your room for the future. Work hard to see good pictures in your mind. The harder you try, the clearer the pictures will be. Are you ready to create a design for the future? All right then, let's start.

➡ First, you will need a window. You may make it any size, shape, or style that you wish to make it. See a picture in your mind of the window that you want . . .
  ➪ Now that you have a window, you have something to look out of . . .
  ➪ When you look out of your window, you'll be able to see whatever you wish to see. What do you wish to see? . . .
  ➪ Look out of your window and see those things . . .
➡ Next, you will need to have a door. Doors come in many shapes, sizes, colors, and designs. Think about the kind of door you wish to have . . .
  ➪ Now, take a good look at the door that you have selected . . .
  ➪ Now that you have a door, you will need to make some decisions about it . . .
  ➪ If you open the door, it will lead to someplace . . .
  ➪ There is something on the other side of the door . . .
  ➪ What do you want it to be? . . .
  ➪ Now open the door and see those things . . .
  ➪ Take a good look . . .
  ➪ Shut the door . . .
➡ You have a window and a door. You need some walls to put them in . . .
  ➪ Your walls may be any color you want them to be . . .
  ➪ If you wish you may select colorful wallpaper . . .
  ➪ See your walls the way you want them to be . . .
  ➪ Do you want pictures or anything else on your walls? . . .
  ➪ Place those things on your walls . . .
➡ It is time to start building your room for the future . . .
  ➪ Take your window and place it in one of the walls . . .

⇨ Stand back and take a look at it . . .

⇨ Take your door and put it in another wall . . .

⇨ Take a good look at your wall and door . . .

⇨ Do you like what you see? . . .

⇨ Make whatever changes you wish to make . . .

➡ Before your room for the future is completed, there is something more to be added. You will need a floor . . .

⇨ How do you wish the floor to appear? . . .

⇨ Think of ways it might appear . . .

⇨ Decide how you wish your floor to appear, then picture it just the way you want it to be . . .

⇨ Walk across the floor . . .

⇨ See a picture of your windows, walls, and door . . .

⇨ Make any changes you wish to make . . .

➡ You now have your room for the future, but it is empty . . .

⇨ Before selecting furnishings for the room, you will need to decide how it is to be used . . .

⇨ What are the many kinds of rooms that it might be? . . .

⇨ Think about this . . .

⇨ Decide, what kind of room it will be . . .

⇨ How will it be used? . . .

⇨ It is time to go shopping for the things that you will use to furnish your room . . .

⇨ Take the furnishings you have selected and arrange them in the room the way you want them to be . . .

⇨ Do you like the arrangement? . . .

⇨ If you wish to make any changes, go ahead and make them . . .

➡ Listen, someone is knocking on the door . . .

⇨ Who might be coming to visit you? . . .

⇨ Open the door and invite them in . . .

⇨ Show the visitors your room for the future and tell them how it is to be used . . .

⇨ It is time for your visitors to leave . . .

⇨ Show them to the door and tell them good-bye . . .

⇨ Now shut the door and turn out the lights . . .

Follow-up activities:

➪ Call on players to give verbal descriptions of their rooms, or parts of their rooms. Call for elaborate, detailed descriptions.

➪ Determine the different kinds of rooms that were selected. Ask players why their rooms will be particularly useful in the future.

➪ Role play the visitor knocking at the door. The selected player will show the visitor about the room describing how the room is to be used.

➪ Call on players to give their room a name. The name may suggest the future and hint at how the room will be used.

Handy Randy, The Space Age Robot

Some people think that the inventor is a strange person. Others believe that he is a genius, and mention the fact that he holds more than 100 patents. Walking to and from his laboratory, he often stops to talk to you. You have found the inventor to be both interesting and friendly. One evening the inventor stops to talk and invites you to visit his laboratory to meet *Handy Randy, the Space Age Robot*.

The next morning you meet the inventor. Together you walk to the laboratory. On the way he tells you that he has succeeded in using alpha waves to computerize the robot's brain. If you know the secret, the robot can be programmed to do anything that people do. It can also float in the air and become invisible.

As you enter the laboratory, you promise that you will keep all secrets that are given to you. The inventor then tells you that when your brain waves are tuned to the robot's signal, the robot will respond to the commands that are given. The inventor also tells you that the robot will become invisible when you send one silent beep. Send two silent beeps and it becomes visible again. You have learned to control the robot.

➡ Now you are ready to meet *Handy Randy* . . .
  ⇨ You are excited . . .
  ⇨ Your heart beats faster . . .
  ⇨ The eventful moment has arrived. You are about to meet *Handy Randy, the Space Age Robot* . . .
  ⇨ Pointing, the inventor tells you that the robot is behind the blue curtain . . .
  ⇨ As he pulls the cord and opens the curtain, there stands *Randy* . . .
  ⇨ Take a good look at him . . .
  ⇨ Tune your brain waves to the robot's signal . . .
  ⇨ The robot is now at your command. Send the message, "Take three steps forward." . . .
  ⇨ Send one silent beep . . .
  ⇨ Send two silent beeps . . .
  ⇨ Command the robot to take three steps backward . . .
  ⇨ Turn off the signal . . .
➡ Your friend tells you that you have done quite well in learning how to command the robot . . .

➪ He then tells you to listen for further instructions . . .

➪ First, whatever you say silently to yourself when you are on the robot's signal, the robot will repeat using your voice . . .

➪ The inventor then tells you that you will be given command of the robot for one week if you promise to make a complete report . . .

➪ You promise to make the report . . .

➡ Now it will be your task to take the robot out of the laboratory and to your home . . .

➪ Think about it . . .

➪ How are you going to do this? . . .

➪ Using your imagination, see yourself taking the robot home with you . . .

➪ Now it is time to write a computerized program for *Randy* . . .

➪ Program the robot to sit at the table when you are eating your evening meal . . .

➪ Remember, *Randy* can be visible or invisible . . .

➪ He can talk using your voice, pass food around the table, and go to the kitchen to bring in anything you might want . . .

➪ In your mind, write the *Evening Meal Program* for the robot . . .

➡ Now it is time to eat and *Randy* is sitting at the table with you . . .

➪ Using your imagination, watch to see what happens . . .

➪ Having completed your meal, you will need to write a *Tomorrow Program* for the robot's computer . . .

➪ Where will you go? . . .

➪ Who will you see? . . .

➪ What will you do? . . .

➪ Include the robot in your plans as you write the program in your mind . . .

➪ It is now tomorrow . . .

➪ Make brain wave contact with the robot and watch to see what happens . . .

➡ *Handy Randy* is like a mechanical twin. Like your shadow, the robot trails along with you wherever you go . . .

➪ Think of some places that you would like to take *Handy Randy* . . .

➪ Maybe a ball game, the zoo, a party, or to the supermarket . . .

➪ Think about the places you would like to take the robot . . .

➪ Choose one of them and write a program in your mind . . .

➪ Now command the robot to perform the program that you have written . . .

⇨ Remember, *Randy* can be visible or invisible . . .

⇨ Watch to see how well he performs . . .

➡ The week is now over. You must return the robot to the laboratory. As you knock on the door, think of the report that you will make to the inventor . . .

Follow-up activities:

⇨ Have the players draw a picture of the robot as they saw it.

⇨ Have players give, or write, a report as they would give it to the inventor.

⇨ Have players write a short story on the topics: *The Day My Robot Left Home Without Me or The Day I Stayed Home and Sent the Robot.*

⇨ Also consider a Robot Play or Robot Model as a follow-up.

2070 Script Writer

A script is an author's copy of a play, novel, movie, broadcast, or telecast. For every story that you read, and every program that you watch, someone has written the story that goes along with the action. Operating behind the scenes, the script writers are the people who create the stories. Using their imagination, they produce clever, interesting, original stories, plays, and programs. You can be a script writer for events to take place in the year *2070*, if you use your imagination. To do this, you will need to project your thinking far into the future, and roam around in your mind for far out ideas and images.

The script that you are about to write will be in four parts. You will think about, and see, the story parts one at a time. After seeing all four parts, you will then go back and join the parts together to form a complete story. If the story parts don't seem to fit as you go along, don't worry about it. If you are ready, turn on your image making machine and we'll go to **Part I.**

➡ Your script for the year *2070* will have to be about someone or something. Your main character may be a person, animal, or a thing . . .

- ➪ In your mind, make a list of the main characters that you wish to consider . . .
- ➪ Now choose the character that you wish to appear in your script, and see that character in great detail . . .
- ➪ Place the picture of your main character in the corner of your mind as we go on to **Part II** of your story . . .

➡ Where do you want your story to take place? It could take place anywhere on earth, at sea, or in space . . .

- ➪ Let your mind drift far and wide as you think about the many places that your story could happen . . .
- ➪ Now choose one of those places . . .
- ➪ Think about the places you would like to take the robot . . .
- ➪ We'll call it the setting . . .
- ➪ See the setting in great detail . . .
- ➪ See it as if you were really there . . .
- ➪ See all there is to see about it . . .
- ➪ Now place the picture of the setting in another corner of your mind as we go on to **Part III** of your story . . .

➡ In the third part of your story, you'll be searching for things that might happen. Of course, in your imagination, anything could happen . . .

⮕ We will call these things events or incidents. An incident is something that could have a serious outcome . . .

⮕ It helps to shape the turn of events. Some examples are: losing your credit cards, being mistaken for a robber, being lost in space, or having the law of gravity repealed . . .

⮕ In your mind, run through some images of unusual incidents that might take place . . .

⮕ Choose one incident that you believe will be different from anything that anyone else will think of . . .

⮕ Got it? See it . . .

⮕ Run it through and watch it take place . . .

⮕ You will come back to the incident later. Right now put it aside as we go on to **Part IV** of your story . . .

➡ Sooner or later, all things come to an end. A story ending tells us how things turned out. Some examples of endings are: The big game was won or lost; the lost treasure was found; a safe rescue was made; or the laser beam finally reached the moon . . .

⮕ Turning on your magic viewer, see some unusual ways in which your story might end . . .

⮕ Don't worry about the rest of the story, just see some endings . . .

⮕ A good ending provides a surprise. Select a surprise ending, then run it through in sound and color in your imagination . . .

➡ You have now written a story script for the year *2070*. As I call out the parts, see them once again . . .

⮕ **Main Character** . . .

⮕ **The Setting** . . .

⮕ **The Incident** that took place . . .

⮕ And last, the **Story Ending** . . .

⮕ Your task now will be to take the parts of the story and weave them together to form a complete script . . .

⮕ If the parts don't fit together, then you will need to find some ways to make them connect . . .

⮕ You can do that by using your imagination . . .

⮕ Take the parts of the story and see it all happen, like a movie in your head . . .

⮕ Remember your script, and be ready to tell or write about it . . .

Follow-up activities:

➪ Call on players to tell, or write about their script.
➪ Have the players use their script to write a play.
➪ Call on players to describe a part of their script; the first player describes the character, the second player describes the setting, etc.
➪ Call on four players to rewrite the script using the data from all four story scripts.

The mind's eye, spontaneously active in dreaming, can also be consciously directed. Unlike the sensory eye, which is bound to the here and now, the mind's eye can travel in space and time to the where and then, can form, probe, and manipulate structures and abstract ideas, can obtain insight into realities that have not been seen, and can foresee future consequences of present plans.

—Robert H. McKim
Experiences in Visual Thinking

Creative Imagination Development

Knowing and understanding the thinking and feeling processes associated with creative expression makes it possible to single out those abilities and focus on their development. Borrowing from the work of Frank E. Williams, the cognitive and affective processes associated with creativity are placed in an interactive mode and illustrated in *The Scamper Model*. The mental manipulations represented by the Scamper techniques are then added to the model and used as a vehicle for process development. In combination, the cognitive and affective processes, plus the idea spurring techniques, provide the foundation and framework upon which the *Scamper* and *Scamper On* games were built.

Cognitive Processes Contributing to Creative Expression

Fluent Thinking
The free flow of thought.
The generation of quantity, the most.
A large number of relevant responses.

Flexible Thinking
Providing for shifts in categories of thought.
Entertaining differing points of view.
Considering alternate plans.

Originality
The production of unusual or unanticipated responses.
Characterized by novelty and uniqueness.
Considering alternate plans.

Elaboration
To refine, embellish, or enrich an idea, plan, or product.
To make a simple idea or response elegant by adding detail.
To provide illuminating, descriptive dimensions.

Affective Processes Contributing to Creative Expression

Curiosity
A strong desire to know about something.
To wonder about, to be inquisitive.
Having the capacity to be puzzled.

Willingness to Take Calculated Risks
Freedom to take a guess, not fearful of being wrong.
Speculation, prediction, and foresight are involved.
Liking the unknown, adventurous.

Preference for Complexity
Likes to bring order out of chaos.
Desires to work with details and knotty problems.
Willingly accepts a challenge.

Intuition
Quick and keen insight.
Plays hunches.
Perceives ideas or information independent of
reasoning processes.

Right Hemisphere Specialization:

Traditionally, education has placed a heavy emphasis on brain functions attributed to the left hemisphere. Creative expression places an emphasis on brain functions attributed to the *right hemisphere*. Highly creative individuals prefer distinct ways of knowing, as described.

- Visual explanations preferred
- Information holistically processed
- Prefers abstract thinking tasks
- Openly expresses emotions
- Prefers to gain general overview
- Uses images to remember
- Ideas are produced intuitively
- Deals with many tasks at once
- Approaches problems playfully
- Likes open, fluid experiences

Scamper Model
for Creative Imagination Development

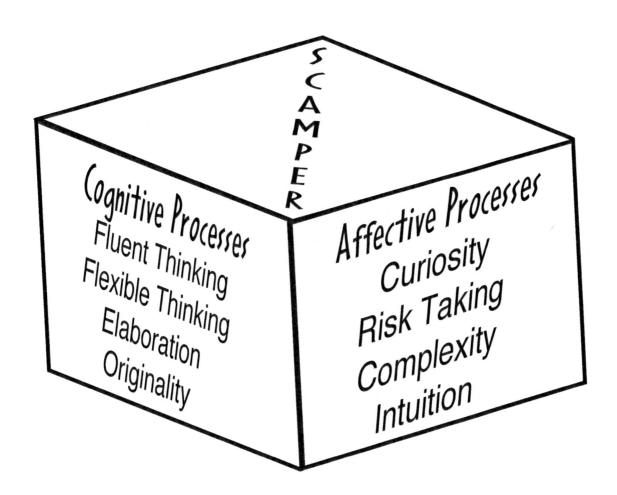

Process reference: Williams, Frank E., *Classroom Ideas for Encouraging Thinking and Feeling*. Buffalo, NY, D.O.K. Publishers, 1970.

Scamper On With Adults

These games have been successfully used with college students enrolled in creative studies courses, and with other adults in training sessions. The *Scamper* techniques have been widely published and applied in the creation of new products. When used with adults, the games have proven to be of value in several ways.

- Gaining involvement of individuals in the group.
- Arousing curiosity and setting levels of expectation.
- Warming up individuals to creative thinking tasks.
- Teaching and practicing the *Scamper* techniques.
- Building and enhancing mental images.
- Applying processes often associated with creative expression.

In gaining these outcomes, adults should be assured that they are not playing fun and games. It may be fun, but it is not for fun! Use of imagery and mental manipulative skills are the common tools of inventors, designers, composers, and artists. The games have proven to be a great leveling activity. All may play. All may contribute ideas and share experiences. All may win, there are no wrong answers. And, as volunteered by a sixth grader, "It's fair for all, nobody can cheat."

Before introducing the games to adults, it is recommended that time be taken to explain the *Scamper Checklist*. The general nature of the checklist, and its use in gaining problem-solving ideas, should be explained. Make it clear that the idea spurring techniques are woven into the games, and that they may be enhanced by playing. Trying improves imagery; it also improves creative expression. Approach adults with the same enthusiasm that you would display with children.

Script for Introducing Scamper On to Adults

Please give me your attention while I introduce you to an activity called *Scamper*. The activity will prompt you to generate unusual ideas and visualize fantastic images. The activities may seem to be fun and games, but I assure you that they are not just for fun! The skills being practiced have application to both your professional and your personal life. I encourage you to participate to the fullest.

➡ Be ready to apply the rules of the activity as I give them to you . . .
⇨ Are you ready? . . .
⇨ Sit with your feet on the floor, and relax in your chair . . .
⇨ You may fold your arms or drape them in your lap . . .
⇨ Listen to the cues as I give them to you . . .
⇨ Generate ideas and see images as directed . . .
⇨ You will be given time to do this . . .
➡ As we prepare to *Scamper* for ideas and images, I have three requests to make . . .
⇨ Dismiss all thoughts that now occupy your mind . . .
⇨ Close your eyes . . .
⇨ Concentrate on the cues as I give them to you . . .
⇨ Fine. We are now ready to *Scamper* . . .

Turn to the practice game Yellow Jello (page 7). Pick up the script on the fourth line with the words, "Pretend that a dish of Jell-O is sitting on the table in front of you." Continue with the balance of the script. After the practice game, proceed to other games of your choice.

Scamper On . . . On Your Own

The *Scamper On* games present a detailed, step-by-step guide designed to bring about vivid and fanciful image-making on the part of those playing the games. For the most part, players are asked to listen to the cues and form mental images. At times, however, players are directed to generate information on their own. This has been done with a purpose in mind. The intent being to encourage players to participate in a *think and then see* process. This is the process that individuals will use when they *Scamper On . . . on their own*. This moves the *Scamper On* process guided fantasy experience to a self-directed fantasy experience. It is important that both leaders and players learn to take charge and guide their own *think and then see* experiences. When this is done, creative image-making may be used to solve problems and meet challenges. Optional activities that follow are designed to extend the *Scamper On* games, and to suggest new and exciting ways of teaching and learning.

Optional Activities for *Scampering* On Your Own

Drama—In playing or replaying the games, instruct players to act out the directions as they are given. This will require some movement on the part of the players as they role play their imaginative experiences. It may be necessary for the leader to formulate some additional roles and to state clear expectations for dramatic activity. This activity may be enhanced by playing background music. Still another twist; using selected recordings, write a script to coordinate with the music. When this is done, players may respond with chorale-type movement. A truly dramatic performance is the result.

Verbal Response—Using this option, the games are played as usual with one exception. At times, the players give a verbal response. The leader will need to explain the procedure to players, explaining that a verbal response may be made to the question, "Who wishes to describe their picture?" or "Who will tell us what they see?" The leader will then call on one of the players who wishes to respond. After one or two responses, the leader then proceeds with the rest of the game. Players should also have the opportunity to share their total experience with others.

This may be done by forming pairs and providing time for each member of the group to describe their experience.

Written Response—Players may be asked to make a written response at the time the games are being played, or after the game has been completed. As you will notice, some of the games call for the generation of ideas. Having each player ready with paper and pencil, the leader will call for a written response by saying, "List your ideas as you think of them." When playing the *Yellow Jello* game, the cue may be "Write down the color that you made your Jell-O and tell what you put in it and on it." This may be done during the game, or after the game has been completed. In many cases, the leader will select a particular scene in the game that is being played. Naming the scene at the close of the game, players are then asked to write a descriptive paragraph giving a detailed account of what they saw in their imagination. It has been found that many players desire to write their own *Scamper On* scripts. In such cases, the leader may encourage the script writers to do it on their own. If help is needed, game titles may be given such as: Coat Hangers, Peanuts, Bricks, Paper Clips, Balloons, Tin Cans, or titles in this book.

As A Role Model—One of the proven ways of encouraging creativity in others, is to model the behavior you wish others to emulate. Anyone in a leadership position has this opportunity. In effect, you are saying, "Do as I do." Listed are ideas that may be implemented by classroom teachers and others. Pick up on these ideas and *Scamper On . . . on your own.*

Idea #1. Use the *Scamper Checklist* to generate problem-solving ideas. Call on others to assist you in the production of creative solutions to everyday problems.

Idea #2. Encourage members of the group to submit topics for brainstorming. In doing so, bring the checklist into play and systematically run through each of the seven questioning categories.*Idea #3.* When members of the group are faced with indecision or confusion, ask "Have you *Scampered* with it?" This may be done, of course, only after the technique has been mastered.

Idea #4. Consider other ways of doing things. Ask yourself, "Other approaches?" "Other methods?" "Other routines?" "Other people?" "Other materials?" "Other outcomes?"

Idea #5. Observe and identify members of the group displaying creative potential. Find ways for them to express their creativity, and encourage them to do so.

Idea #6. Recognize and reward creative expression wherever and whenever it is observed.

Drawing
The Intelligence-Intellect Distinction

Way Beyond the IQ Using this provocative title, J. P. Guilford makes reference to the discoveries which have contributed greatly to an improved understanding of the nature of human intellect. Commenting on the narrowness of the IQ as a measure of ability, Dr. Guilford has this to say:

> "Instead of looking at intelligence as one general resource for understanding and problem-solving, measurable by a single value, the IQ or intelligence quotient, we now see that it is composed of a very large number of distinct abilities or functions. Since we know about the various functions and what they are like, we are prepared to do something about them."

Indeed, we are prepared to do something about them. Guilford's *Structure of Intellect Model* (S.O.I.) provides us with principles that contribute greatly to the understanding and control of mental operations. While the IQ may be regarded as a predictor of success for formal education, the S.O.I. Model is all inclusive of known mental capacities. Unfortunately, the focus of formal education is on the development of a limited number of mental abilities measured by intelligence tests.

If the scope of formal education were to go beyond the IQ and draw the intelligence-intellect distinction, attention could then be given to the roles played by intellectual abilities in daily life. Attention could also be given to the skills involved in problem-solving and creative thinking. The Range of Mental Ability draws the Intelligence-Intellect Distinction.

Range of Mental Ability

Creativity: A. Revising the Known.

B. Exploring the Undetermined.

C. Constructing What Might Be.

I
N
T
E
L
L
E
C
T

Intelligence: A. Retaining the Known.

B. Learning the Predetermined.

C. Conserving What It Is.

Low   ⟵   I.Q.   ⟶   High

References and Resources
for
Imagery and Creativity

Arnheim, Rudolph. *Visual Thinking*. Los Angeles: The University of California Press.

Biondi, Angelo M. (Ed.) *Have an Affair With Your Mind*. Great Neck, NY: Creative Synergetic Associates, Ltd.

DeBono, Edward E. *Lateral Thinking, Creativity Step by Step*. New York: Harper & Row.

Eberle, Bob. *Apple Shines, Polishing Student Writing Skills*. Carthage, IL: Good Apple, Inc.

Eberle, Bob. *Chip In, Motivational Activities to Stimulate Better Thinking*. Carthage, IL: Good Apple Inc.

Eberle, Bob and Stanish, Bob. *CPS for Kids: A Resource Book for Teaching Creative Problem-Solving to Children*. Waco, TX: Prufrock Press.

Eberle, Bob. *Help for Solving Problems Creatively at Home and School*. Carthage, IL: Good Apple Inc.

Edwards, Betty. *Drawing on the Right Side of the Brain*. Los Angeles: J. P. Tarcher Inc.

Elwell, Patricia A., and Treffinger, Donald J., (Eds.) *CPS for Teens, Classroom Activities for Teaching Creative Problem Solving*. Waco, TX: Prufrock Press.

Gorden, W. J. J. *Synectics*. New York: Harper & Row.

Gowan, John Curtis. *Development of the Creative Individual*. San Diego, CA: Knapp Publishers.

Gowan, John Curtis. *Trance, Art, and Creativity*. Buffalo, NY: The Creative Education Foundation.

Guilford, J. P. *The Nature of Human Intelligence*. New York: McGraw-Hill.

Guilford, J. P. *Way Beyond the I.Q.* Buffalo, NY: The Creative Education Foundation.

McIntosh, Joel E., and Meacham, April W. *Creative Problem Solving in the Classroom*. Waco, Tx: Prufrock Press.

McKim, Robert H. *In Search of Human Effectiveness, Identifying and Developing Creativity*. Buffalo, NY: The Creative Education Foundation.

Noller, Ruth B., Treffinger, Donald J., and Houseman, Elwood D. *It's A Gas to be Gifted, or CPS for the Gifted and Talented*. Buffalo, NY: D.O.K. Publishers Inc.

Noller, Ruth B. *Scratching the Surface of Creative Problem Solving, A Bird's Eye View of CPS*. Buffalo, NY: D.O.K. Publishers Inc.

Ornstein, R. *The Psychology of Consciousness*. 2nd Edition. New York: Harcourt Brace Jovanovich.

Osborn, Alex F. *Applied Imagination*. 3rd Edition. New York: Scribners.

Parnes, Sidney J. *Creativity: Unlocking Creative Potential*. Buffalo, NY: D.O.K. Publishers Inc.

Parnes, Sidney J. *The Magic of Your Mind*. Buffalo, NY: The Creative Education Foundation in association with Bearly Limited.

Rugg, Harold. *Imagination*. New York: Harper & Row.

Renzulli, Joseph S. *New Directions in Creativity*. Volumes Mark 1, Mark 2, and Mark 3. New York: Harper & Row.

Samuels, Mike, and Samuels, Nancy. *Seeing with the Mind's Eye*. New York: Random House Books.

Shallcross, Doris J. *Teaching Creative Behavior*. Englewood Cliffs, NJ: Prentice-Hall.

Stanish, Bob, and Eberle, *Bob. Be A Problem-Solver*. Waco, TX: Prufrock Press.

Stanish, Bob. Sunflower: *Thinking, Feeling, Doing Activities for Creative Expression*. Carthage, IL: Good Apple Inc.

Torrance, E. Paul. *The Search for Satori and Creativity*. Buffalo, NY: The Creative Education Foundation.

Williams, Frank E. *Classroom ideas for Encouraging Thinking and Feeling*. Buffalo, NY: D.O.K. Publishers Inc.